Stars & Stars

Written by Rae Cuda
Photography by Rae and Trisha Cuda

Thanks to the Creator of real stars, real children, and real imagination.

Star

Open, Empty
Window, Hole, Nothing

Star

Pointed, Sharp
Spur, Boot, Round

Star

Bright, Night
Twinkle, Far, Many

Star

Shiny, Polished
Ship, Wheel, Steer

Star

Button, Red
Jeans, Fasten, Sewn

Star

Waving, Fluttering
Flag, Flying, Home

Star

Grate, Sidewalk
Rusty, Metal, Drain

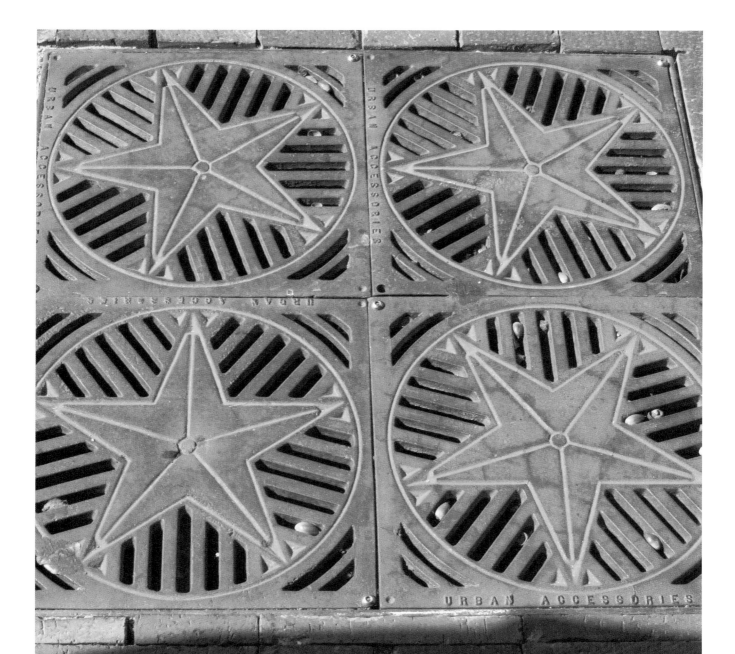

Star

Important, Chosen
Student, Honor, Special

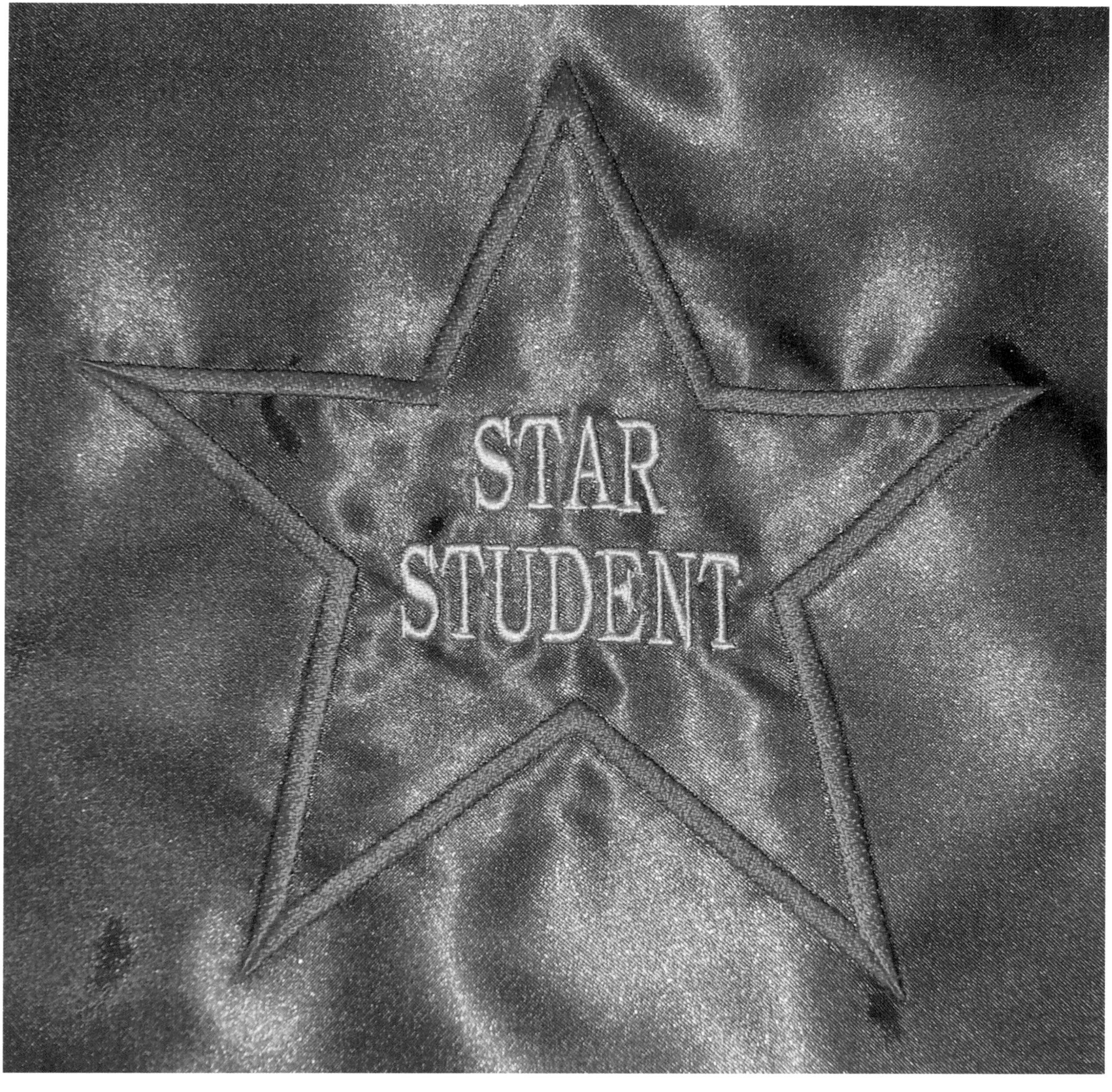
STAR
STUDENT

Star

Piñata, Party
Candy, Break, Fun

Star

Treat, Sweet
Cookie, Frosted, Yummy

Star

Burning, Glowing
Flame, Shining, Warm

Star

Living, Fish
Bumpy, Ocean, Swimming

What about YOU?

Where do you see stars? Can you see the stars in the sky from where you live? It's hard to see the stars at night in a city, and easy to see them in the country where there is less light from streets.

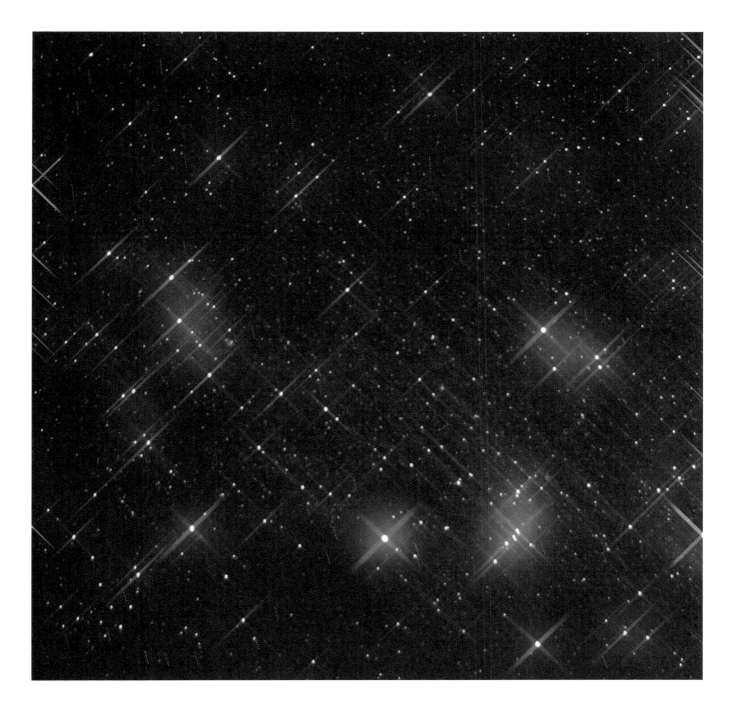

Where do you see the shape of a star?

Look for them on signs, on buildings.

Look for stars on fabric or metal.

You might have star stickers on a chart at school or home!

If you break a dry cottonwood twig, you can see a star inside!

Find as many stars as you can. You can watch for them when you ride in the car or shop in a store.

Stars are everywhere!

Made in the USA
Charleston, SC
14 April 2015